This material was previously published in the
book *Mini Quilts* (ISBN: 978-1-62113-796-2)
First published in this format 2015

The Taunton Press
Inspiration for hands-on living®

The Taunton Press, Inc.
63 South Main Street, PO Box 5506
Newtown, CT 06470-5506
e-mail: tp@taunton.com

Executive Editor, Series: Shawna Mullen
Assistant Editor, Series: Timothy Stobierski
Series Art Director: Rosalind Loeb Wanke
Copy editor: Candace B. Levy
Photographers: Alexandra Grablewski; (p. 28);
Scott Phillips (pp. 6, 10, 14, 18, 22); Jodie &
Jayne Davis (pp. 2–5, 8–9, 12–13, 16–17, 20–21,
24–27, 29)
Illustrator: Jeffrey Rey

Threads® is a trademark of The Taunton
Press, Inc., registered in the U.S. Patent and
Trademark Office.

The following names/manufacturers
appearing in *Fabulous Mini Quilts* are
trademarks: Aurifil™, Lite Steam-A-Seam2®

Library of Congress Cataloging-in-
Publication Data in progress

ISBN 978-1-63186-130-7

CONTENTS

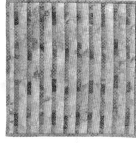

Making the Quilt

THE SCANT ¼-IN. SEAM ALLOWANCE

A seam allowance is the width of fabric between the stitched line and the raw edge. Traditionally, a seam allowance in quilting is ¼ in. since a wider seam allowance in piecing would just create unnecessary bulk.

Your machine has a ¼-in. presser foot and a line on the throat plate, so why worry about the ¼ in.? Because, as famous quilting instructor Mary Ellen Hopkins used to say, we all have our own personal ¼-in. seam allowance.

The ¼-in. is different, depending on the way we sew and the tools we use. This fact may be the reason our quilt blocks turn out a little short or a bit too large. Even a slightly off ¼ in. seam allowance can become substantial when magnified over all of the blocks in a quilt.

What we try to achieve in our piecing is a scant ¼-in. seam. The *scant* part of the equation is what makes up for the turn in the fabric when you press your seam allowances to one side or press them open. If we sew a perfect ¼ in., it becomes more than ¼ in. when we press.

SEWING A ¼-IN. SEAM

PIECING PRESSER FOOT METHOD

If you're using a presser foot made for piecing, you can adjust how you are aligning your fabric as you sew. As you stitch, align the fabric just a hair to the left of the right edge of the ¼-in. foot. This will give the pieces you are joining that scant breathing room.

STACKED TAPE GUIDE METHOD

If you prefer not to rely on eyeballing your scant ¼-in. seam, try this method.

1. Lay a rotary cutting ruler under the presser foot so the needle will go down at the ¼-in. mark. Check the position by lowering the needle by hand just shy of the ruler (see the photo below).

2. Stick a 1-in. piece of masking tape to the bed of the machine, aligning it along the right-hand edge of the ruler. Sew a test, adjusting the tape as necessary. Once you have the placement correct, build up the stack of tape to form a ridge to butt your patchwork pieces against as you sew.

THE ¼-IN. SEAM TEST

Here's a test to try that just may surprise you. In fact, do it during your next sew-in with your friends. You'll be amazed at how many different ¼-in. seam allowances there will be!

Cut three pieces of fabric, each 2 in. by 3 in. Sew them together along their long edges using a ¼-in. seam allowance. Press the seam allowances to one side. Measure the width of the center strip. It should measure 1½ in. If your seam allowance was a perfect (or, actually, scant) ¼ in., you're a pro! If not, you discovered why your blocks are turning out small.

SQUARING UP YOUR MINI QUILT

Before binding your quilt, you need to make sure it's the right size. Squaring up is a very important last step in constructing quilt blocks. Let's say you are making a quilt of 10-in. blocks that is six blocks wide and six blocks tall. If some or all of your block measurements are off even a little, your entire quilt will be off.

That said, if all the blocks are consistently ¼ in. too large, your quilt will simply be larger than anticipated. As long as you're consistent, you should be okay.

All the mini quilts in this book are designed to be 16 in. square, with an extra ½ in. square for binding. When you finish your project, measure its height and width. If it's a little wonky—say 16⅓ in. by 16¾ in.— then make the mini 16⅓ in. square. But if the quilt is 16¼ in. square, it's already square and won't be joined to another piece, so don't fret.

If your mini quilt is not 16 in. square before binding, see if you can figure out why. Is it your piecing? Did your quilting draw up the fabric? It's all about learning from your mistakes!

Always square up your quilted mini before binding. Here's how: lay the mini on your cutting mat. You'll quickly see any offending edges. Use your rotary cutter, cutting mat, and see-through ruler to carefully trim the quilt into a perfect square.

BINDING SMALL QUILTS

Throughout this booklet, a regular double-fold straight-of-grain binding is used. This is the binding most often used by quilters. It gives a strong, neat finish and wears well, which is very important for a quilt that is used frequently, such as a bed quilt. Instructions for the traditional double-fold binding are here.

For the mini quilts you will need only two strips of fabric: 2¼ in. wide by the length of your fabric (typically, 42 in. to 45 in.). Packaged double-fold binding is available to buy, but the fabric will often be a different quality from your quilt fabric, resulting in a less-than-professional-looking finished project. Plus, it's so simple to make your own binding!

DOUBLE-FOLD BINDING

1. Cut the ends of the strips at a 45-degree angle. Match the short end of one strip to the short end of the other strip. Seam.

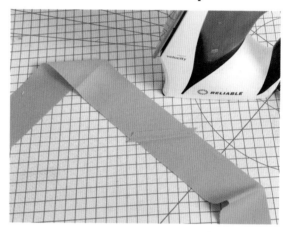

2. Press the seam open. Press the strip in half lengthwise.

3. Begin stitching the binding to the quilt edge halfway between two corners. Leave a 6-in.-long tail at the top before starting to stitch. Stop and backstitch ¼ in. from the bottom corner.

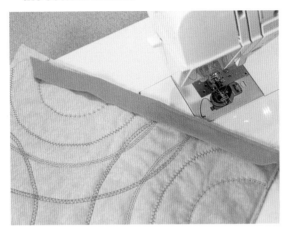

4. Turn the quilt. Fold up the binding strip vertically.

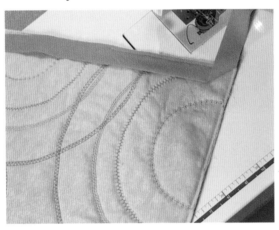

5. Fold the binding down. Starting at the top raw edge of the quilt, stitch, backstitch, and continue stitching down to the next corner. Stop ¼ in. from the edge and backstitch again.

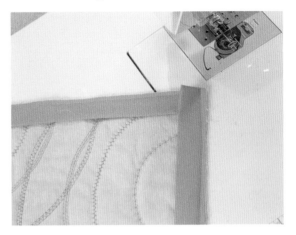

6. Repeat for the remaining corners. When you return to the side you started on, stitch the binding to the first few inches of that edge.

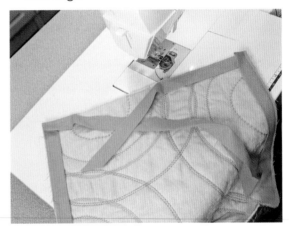

7. Overlap the ends of the binding. Trim so they overlap 2¼ in.

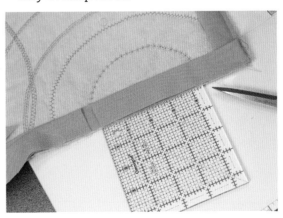

8. Open the left strip and turn.

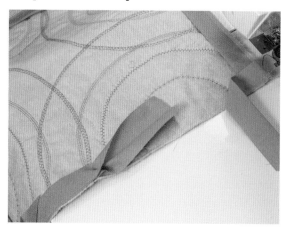

9. Open the right strip.

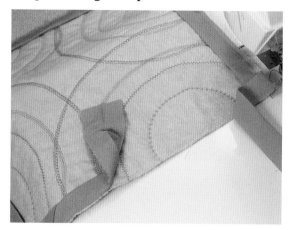

10. Mark a 45-degree line on the right strip. Match the strips perpendicularly, right sides together. Pin. Stitch on the line.

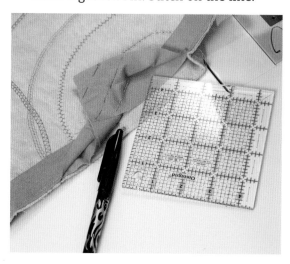

11. Trim the binding edges. Press the seam allowance open.

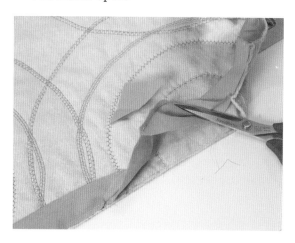

12. Refold the binding. Press. Finish the stitching on the edge of the quilt.

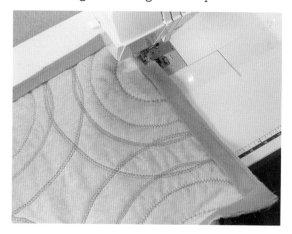

13. Turn the binding to the back of the quilt and pin in place. Hand-stitch the binding using a blind stitch. This stitch gives a neat, finished look in the back.

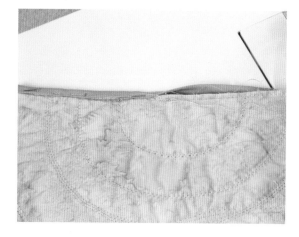

THE DESIGN: Interlocking circles are a familiar theme in quilting. The Double Wedding Ring pattern is the first example that comes to mind; it's an all-time favorite of many quilters, myself included. When designing this project, I played on a similar image of interwoven circles. At first I drafted a symmetrical design, but then I mixed it up by setting it a bit out of alignment.

Decorative
STITCHED CIRCLES

DESIGNER: Jodie Davis

How many great decorative stitches does your sewing machine have? Have you ever used those stitches? Let this project be your excuse! You can customize the design by choosing your stitches, thread colors, textures, and of course, your fabric. I found this cotton damask-type fabric in my stash. Because it goes well with the couch in my den, I created the mini quilt with the intention of turning it into a pillow later. (For instructions for making the pillow, see Mini Quilt Pillow, on p. 28.)

SKILL LEVEL: Easy | THE TECHNIQUE: Decorative stitches

What You'll Need

- **Decorative Stitched Circles template (p. 30)**
- **Fat quarter of fabric for the quilt top**
- **Fat quarter fabric for the backing**
- **¼ yd. fabric for the binding**
- **17½-in.-square batting**
- **Four colors of thread for decorative stitching**

NOTE: Because you'll need to run the stitches past the 16-in. square, I have allowed extra fabric to stop and start on. You'll get a nice decorative stitch going before stitching on the quilt top, which will be invisible when finished.

What You'll Learn

If you are a pretty good sewing machine driver, this project will be easy. This mini involves drawing circles on your quilt top and then steering around them.

Choosing Thread

For this project, I used a 40-weight cotton Mako from Aurifil™ in the bobbin and as my top thread. Check your machine to see if you need to change your upper thread tension. Test rayon, metallic, and even wool thread to see what works. You can also pick a heavier thread weight; in fact, I have doubled 50-weight thread, running it from two spools and into a size 90 needle, when I've needed a heftier effect. Make a little test quilt sandwich and try out your stitches and thread before sewing on your quilt.

Fabric Cutting Chart

Cut your fabric according to this chart.

Fabric	Measurements	No. of Pieces
Quilt Top	17½" square	1
Backing	17½" square	1
Binding	2¼" by 42" to 45"	2

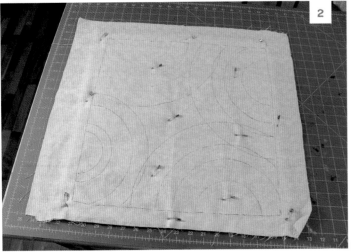

TRACE THE CIRCLES

1. Copy the Decorative Stitched Circles template on p. 30, and enlarge it by 400 percent one quarter of the pattern at a time. Tape the pattern together. Transfer the circle designs to the fabric using the tracing method of your choice. Mark the outer edge of the finished 16-in. square too, so you'll know where to start and stop your stitching.

QUILT

2. Follow the instructions on p. 13 to make a quilt sandwich.

NOTE: If you'd like, use scraps of fabric to make a practice mini quilt sandwich so you can test your stitches before committing to your real quilt. Experiment with the different stitches on your machine. You may wish to loosen your top tension, which hides your bobbin thread and gives a smoother-looking stitch, but most likely that won't be necessary.

Tip Layering the quilt sandwich before stitching the circles eliminates the need for a stabilizer. If you were to sew the circles on just the quilt top, you would need something to stabilize the fabric. The method used here allows the decorative stitching to show on the back. Mine looks great, so it's not a problem. If you choose a different fabric from that on the front, you could have a reversible quilt!

3. Wind bobbins with each of the threads you'll be using to stitch the circles. Choose a presser foot that will allow you to see your traced line well. An open-toe appliqué foot works well, though your regular sewing foot may be your favorite.

Choose the thread color and style of stitch you wish to use for the outer, largest circles.

Start your stitching about ½ in. outside the markings designating the 16-in. square. Stitch along the traced line, gently following the curve.

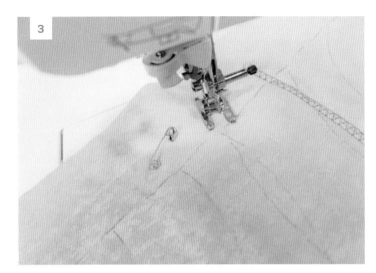

4. As you complete stitching the arc, continue about ½ in. past the traced line that indicates the edge of the 16-in. square, sewing into the seam allowance. Sew each of the largest arcs.

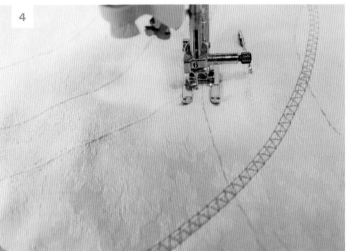

5. Switch thread and change your sewing machine to the decorative stitch you've chosen for the next smaller circles and stitch. Repeat for the last two sets of arcs. Baste along the outer edge of the quilt, ⅛ in. outside of the marked edge, which designates the 16-in. edge. Trim to 16½ in. square.

BIND

6. If you are binding the quilt, make a continuous binding from the 2¼-in. wide strips of fabric. Then bind the quilt as instructed on p. 3.

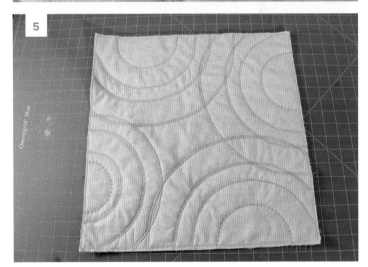

THE DESIGN: Inspiration is all around us. All we have to do is open our eyes. I like linear shapes. No matter how ancient the object, it has a modern look to me. See the way the bricks are laid in a wall? That's a linear design. A rusty heating grate was the inspiration for this quilt. I saw sunshine and shadows and that brief period when they blend together day after day.

Picky Piecing
MODERN GRAPHIC QUILT

DESIGNER: Jayne Davis

I guess you could call me a picky piecer. I like seams to join exactly and lines to be straight. Remember the old saying, "Anything worth doing is worth doing well"? I'm a firm believer. Fabric is not cheap, and your time has value. If you're going to spend all that money and time making a quilt, you should be picky about your piecing. With this mini quilt, you'll become an expert at precision piecing. Here is an opportunity to hone your skills and find that it doesn't take all that much extra effort to do the job right.

SKILL LEVEL: Intermediate │ THE TECHNIQUE: Chainstitching

What You'll Need

- ¾ yd. light colored batik fabric (A) for the wide strips and backing
- Fat quarter blue batik fabric (B) for the pieced strips and binding
- Fat eighth brown batik fabric (C) for the pieced strips
- Scrap orange fabric (D) for highlights in the pieced strips
- 21-in. by 20-in. batting

What You'll Learn

You will be working with small pieces of fabric to create a striking graphic design. Chainstitching is the fastest way to piece the strips.

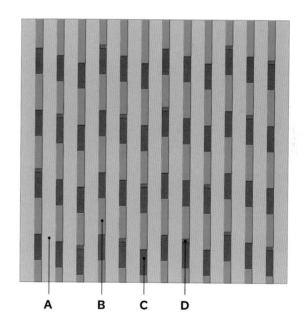

A   B   C   D

Fabric Cutting Chart

Cut your fabric according to this chart.

	Fabric	Measurements	No. of Pieces
FOR THE BACKING	A	21" by 20"	1
THE WIDE STRIPS	A	1½" by 18"	13
FOR THE BINDING	B	2¼" by 20"	4
FOR THE PIECED STRIPS	B	1" by 3"	60
	C	1" by 2¼"	48
	D	1" square	15

PIECE THE STRIPS

1. Start piecing with fabric D. Take a 1-in. piece of blue fabric B and lay it right side up. Fold an orange fabric D piece in half lengthwise with wrong sides facing and line it up with the short, top edge of fabric B, raw edges together. Top with a brown fabric C piece right side down, making sure the top raw edges are all even. Machine stitch. Repeat until all the orange fabric D pieces are used. Cut these 15 chained pieces apart and set aside.

   Next, chainstitch the 1-in. blue fabric B pieces and the remaining brown fabric C pieces in pairs. You'll have 12 blue fabric B pieces left. Cut the chained pieces apart.

SEW THE STRIPS TOGETHER

2. Sew these elements together to make the pieced strips. Follow the drawing on p. 11 to distribute the highlight pieces. End each strip with one of the remaining 1-in. blue fabric B pieces. Press the seams toward the dark fabric, making sure the folded edge of each fabric D piece turns up and covers the fabric B piece.

3. Stitch all the pieces together following drawing on p. 11.

   Begin joining the light fabric A strips and the pieced strips. Separate the pieced strips into 3 groups. Cut ½ in. off the top edge of the strips in group 1. Cut ¼ in. off the top edge of group 2. Do nothing to group 3. Join the strips as shown in the drawing, alternating among the groups of pieced strips so the colors ripple. After each seam is sewn, stop and press the seam toward the light strip.

QUILT AND BIND

4. Once all the strips are sewn together, make a quilt sandwich (see below). To quilt, begin in the center and work outward. Stitch in the light fabric A strip very close to each side of the pieced strip, but do not stitch directly in the seamline.

5. Using your rotary cutter, trim the quilt to 16 in. square.

6. If you are binding the quilt, make a continuous binding from the 2¼-in. wide strips of blue fabric B. Then bind the quilt as instructed on p. 3.

A Quilt Sandwich

By definition, a quilt is two pieces of fabric—the quilt top and the backing—with something soft in between. To get that soft layer, quilters use batting.

A quilt sandwich consists of the three layers that are quilted together: a quilt top, batting, and backing. Packaged battings are readily available at your local quilt shop, fabric store, and online. You'll find a wide range of fiber content, such as cotton, polyester, wool, and silk and combinations of all these.

To build your quilt sandwich, start from the bottom layer and work up. There are three ways to hold the layers together: basting spray, safety pins, and hand basting. Is one method better than another? Not really. Try them all and see what works best for you.

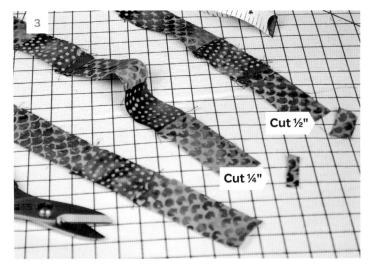

Cut ½"

Cut ¼"

THE DESIGN: Inspired by Hawaiian quilts, this mini quilt quickly turned into a more modern interpretation. Hawaiian quilts are gorgeous examples of handwork mastery. Extremely simple in design, a shape is usually made out of a solid-color fabric and appliquéd to a plain background, which is most often white or cream. The result is simple and graphic.

Hawaiian Gone Modern
STENCILED QUILT

DESIGNER: Jodie Davis

For this project I applied paint to fabric using stencils for a nice clean effect. Stencils are quick and easy to cut and so much faster than appliqué. As long as you don't glob your paint on, the fabric will not be stiff. It will take you no time to become proficient at fabric painting. In fact, this may be the easiest project in the booklet. Stenciling results in a mark-of-the-hand look that appliqué doesn't offer. With so many mass-produced products out there, something made by human hands is appreciated that much more. I also turned this pattern into a pillow (see p. 28).

SKILL LEVEL: Easy | THE TECHNIQUES: Stenciling on fabric, hand embroidery running stitch

What You'll Need

- Hawaiian Gone Modern Stenciled Quilt templates (p. 31)
- Fat quarter high-quality gold quilters' cotton for the quilt top
- Fat quarter gold fabric for the backing
- ¼ yd. green fabric for the binding
- 16½-in.-square batting
- White embroidery floss to outline the stencils
- Spray fixative (optional)
- Stencil plastic or file folders for the templates
- 5 bottles acrylic paint in various colors
- Stencil brush, natural sponge, or other special paint applicator

What You'll Learn

Create your own fabric design by making a stencil and applying acrylic paint to fabric using a sponge. Then, after creating the quilt sandwich, add detail using embroidery floss and a simple running stitch.

Fabric Cutting Chart

Cut your fabric according to this chart.

Fabric	Measurements	No. of Pieces
Quilt top	16½" square	1
Backing	16 " square	1
Binding	2¼" by 42" to 45"	2

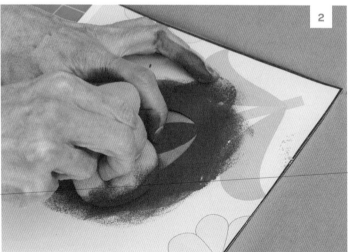

STENCIL

1. Copy the two Hawaiian Gone Modern Stenciled Quilt templates on p. 31 and enlarge the red flower by 400 percent and the yellow flower by 200 percent. Trace the pattern onto the stencil plastic, using your favorite technique. Cut the stencil shapes as designated on the pattern, creating a separate stencil for each color. Leave the other areas marked for placement.

   To create placement lines for your stenciling, fold the quilt top fabric in half and in half again. Press. On each line, make a dot 2¾ in. down from the raw edge. This marks the placement for the center of the yellow flower.

2. Starting with whichever stencil you wish, line up the edge of the stencil to the folded lines so that it will appear in one-quarter of the quilt top. Dab the sponge or brush into the paint, then onto a paper towel. You want it to be fairly dry so the paint doesn't run under the stencil. Dab gently into the area to be painted, building the color gradually.

3. Repeat step 2 for the remaining quarters of the quilt. Then repeat for the remaining stencils. For the yellow flower, line it up as indicated on the stencil template with the center on your dot. Stencil the entire flower and then the red circle on top.

Tip Test on scrap fabric first. You will get the feel for how much paint to load onto your stenciling tool. If you find your stencil slipping as you dab, you can use a temporary spray fixative on the underside of the stencil to hold it in place.

QUILT AND BIND

4. Lay the backing fabric wrong side up on a table and make a quilt sandwich (p. 13).

5. Work a running stitch with the embroidery floss around the design elements, starting and ending with a square knot on the back of the work or buried in the backing.

6. Continue to work a running stitch around all four squares.

7. If you are binding the quilt, make a continuous binding from the 2¼-in. wide strips of fabric. Then bind the quilt as instructed on p. 3.

THE DESIGN: The fabric is the star here, so keep the design simple. I chose to make this mini quilt from sixteen 4½-in. squares, half a light color (in this instance white) and half a dark color (a deep rich red). To add a little extra interest, I added a contrasting circle at each intersection topped with a button. For the backing and binding, I chose a paisley cotton that picks up the wool colors. All the layers are tied together through the buttons.

ALL TIED UP IN WOOL

DESIGNER: Jayne Davis

The feel of wool conjures up walks in the woods and cozy evenings by the fire. It warms our bodies, and it's a tactile fiber that feels just plain cuddly to the touch. So I decided to make a mini quilt out of wool and tie the quilt together rather than quilt it with stitches. Then I added a button or two for pizzazz.

SKILL LEVEL: Easy | **THE TECHNIQUES:** Working with wool, tying a quilt, embellishing a quilt with buttons

What You'll Need

- **All Tied Up in Wool template (p. 30)**
- ¼ yd. dark-colored wool
- ¼ yd. light-colored wool
- 8-in.-square black wool
- ⅔ yd. cotton fabric for the backing and binding (this fabric should pick up the wool colors used)
- 18-in.-square batting
- 1 sheet fusible web such as Lite Steam-A-Seam2®
- 1 skein six-strand cotton embroidery floss to match the dark wool
- 1 skein black six-strand cotton embroidery floss
- 1 medium embroidery needle
- 1 large tapestry needle
- 9¾-in. or 1-in. buttons with two holes
- Pressing cloth, such as a white cotton dish cloth

What You'll Learn

You'll become comfortable working with wool. You'll also hone your skills in stitching a simple hand-embroidered blanket stitch. With this mini quilt, you'll be tying through buttons for an added touch—and it's much faster than quilting!

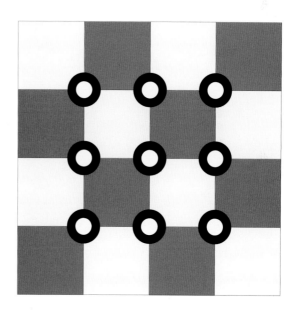

Fabric Cutting Chart

Cut your fabric according to this chart.

	Fabric	Measurements	No. of Pieces
FOR THE SQUARES	Dark wool	4½" square	8
	Light wool	4½" square	8
FOR THE BACKING	Backing fabric	18" square	1
FOR THE BINDING	Binding fabric	2¼" by 42" to 45"	2

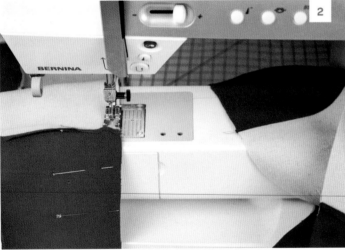

PREPARE THE PATTERN

1. Using the 2-in. All Tied Up in Wool template on p. 30, trace nine circles onto the fusible web following the manufacturer's directions.

   Again, following manufacturer's directions, remove the paper backing and finger-press the circles onto the wrong side of the black wool.

   Cut out the circles along the traced lines.

2. Chainstitch the 4½-in. squares together following the sequence shown in the lay-out drawing on p. 19. Begin by stitching a dark and light square together. Then chainstitch two of these units together. You'll have four strips of four squares each.

   Press the seams open. When you turn the strips over and press the seams on the right side, use a pressing cloth.

   Tip It's important to use a pressing cloth with wool, because the high heat needed to make steam can scorch or leave a shine on the fabric.

Following the layout drawing, stitch the rows together. Carefully press the seams open.

3. Remove the backing from the fusible web and place each black circle on the checkerboard, as shown in the drawing on p. 19. Finger-press them in place and then fuse them in following the manufacturer's directions. Don't forget to use a pressing cloth.

Tip Place the iron down and lift it up when fusing. Don't move it back and forth as you would when ironing.

4. Blanket-stitch around each circle by hand or machine. Stitch as close to the edge as possible.

ATTACH THE BUTTONS

5. Make a quilt sandwich (p. 13), centering your mini quilt on the batting. Thread the tapestry needle with all six strands of the dark embroidery floss and stitch a button in the middle of each circle.

To finish, pull the floss taut and cut it off at about 3 in. long. Tie the ends in a firm square knot. Trim the thread ends to ½ in.

6. Carefully trim the tied quilt to 16-in. square. If you are binding the quilt, make a continuous binding from the 2¼-in. strips of fabric. Then bind the quilt as instructed on p. 3.

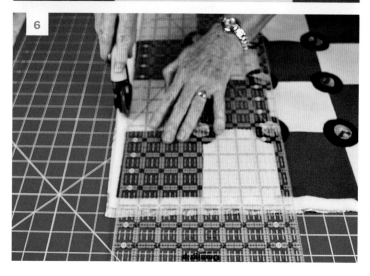

THE DESIGN: To accentuate the scallops, this quilt is put together using the pillowcase method rather than being layered into a quilt sandwich, quilted, and bound. The backing and quilt top are sewn right sides together on top of the batting, while the stitched and turned scallops are simply inserted into the seams of the quilt top as it is sewn together. Then the quilt is turned right side out and the seam is hand closed, eliminating the need for a binding.

SCALLOPED!

DESIGNER: Jodie Davis

This quilt explores a very simple example of a design element you can use in your quilts as either a border or as three-dimensional texture. In this case, scallops are used both ways. The scallops are sewn, turned, and pressed and then inserted into the seams of the quilt top. Plus a row is stitched into the seam at the outside edges of the sides of the quilt.

SKILL LEVEL: Intermediate | THE TECHNIQUE: Inserted design element

What You'll Need

- Scalloped! template on p. 30
- Fat eighth red fabric for the quilt top
- Fat eighth pink fabric for the quilt top
- ⅓ yd. cream fabric for the scallops
- Fat quarter fabric for the backing
- 14½-in. by 16½-in. batting
- Air- or water-dissolving pen
- Smoothly pointed turning tool (optional)

What You'll Learn

For this design you will stitch scalloped strips, then insert them into the seams as you construct the quilt top.

NOTE: The scallops on the sides of the quilt make it finish at 16 in. square.

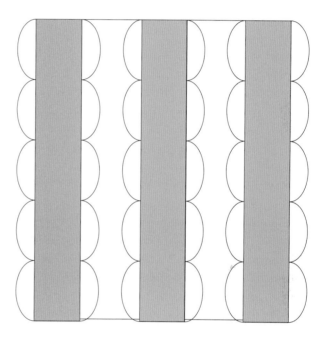

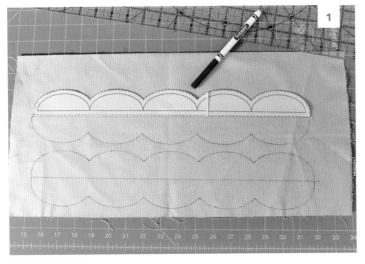

Fabric Cutting Chart

Cut your fabrics according to this chart.

Fabric	Measurements	No. of Pieces
Red	3" by 16½"	3
Pink	3¾" by 16½"	2
Backing	16½" by 14½"	2

TRACE THE SCALLOPS

1. Following instructions on p. 30, make three copies of the Scalloped! template and enlarge by 200 percent. Cut along the dashed lines. Tape the pattern together, omitting one scallop from the last template to form five scallops. Fold the cream fabric in half lengthwise. Lay the template on top of the doubled fabric and trace the scallops using an air- or water-dissolving pen. Trace another group of scallops, placing the template next to the first traced scallops to form a mirror image. Continue tracing until you have six groups of scallops.

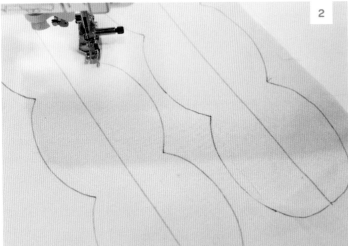

STITCH THE SCALLOPS

2. Beginning and ending with a backstitch, sew a strip of scallops along the curved edge using a ¼-in. seam allowance. Repeat for all six of the scallop pieces.

3. Cut along the straight line. Trim the seam allowance along the scalloped edges to about ⅛ in. Clip into the inside Vs up to the seam to help the curve lay flat when turned right side out. Do not clip past the seamline.

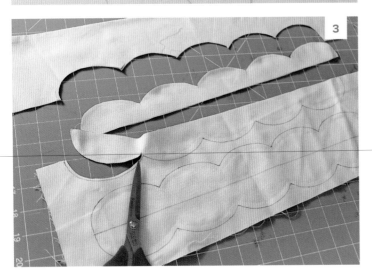

FINISH THE SCALLOPS

4. Turn the scallop pieces right side out. For perfectly smooth curved edges, use a smoothly pointed turning tool to push the edges out from the inside. Run the tool along the seam a few times to push it all the way out, smoothing it into a perfect curve.

SEW THE QUILT TOP

5. Match a scallop to one long edge of a right-side-up red strip. The scallop will stop short of the corners by ¼ in. Stitch the scallop in place along the length of the strip.

6. Match a scallop to the other edge of the red strip. Pin it in place.

Get in Shape

In addition to scallops, you can insert folded triangles into seams. Or even simpler, folded strips of fabric. Quilters often use the latter as a way to add a second inside border to a quilt, which lends a small strip of color to bring out a color in one of the fabrics in the design. This type of edging can make a big difference in making a quilt sing.

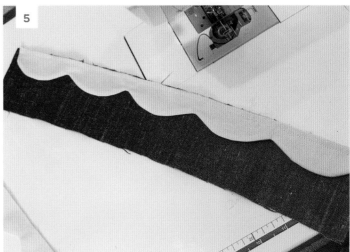

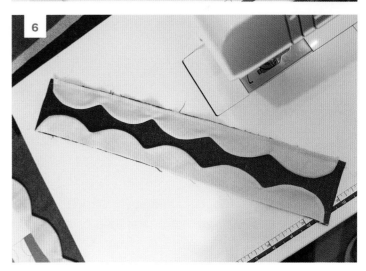

7. Place a pink strip on top, right side down, matching the raw edges of the strip you just finished.

8. Stitch the long edge of the pink strip to the scallop strip.

9. Place the straight edge of a scallop strip against the right-side edge of the pink strip. Place a red strip right side down on top of the scallop. The pink and red strips will be right sides together.

10. Sew the pink strip, scallop strip, and red strip together along the edge.

11. Repeat steps 6 to 10 until you have used all three red strips and both pink strips. Press the interior scallops toward the pink strips, leaving the two outside scallops folded in for now.

LAYER AND STITCH THE QUILT

12. To eliminate the need for binding and to put the scallops center stage along the edge of the quilt, use the pillowcase method. Here's how.

Place the batting on your work surface. Place the quilt top right side up on top of the batting. Place the quilt backing right side down on the quilt top, matching the edges. Pin the layers in place along the edges.

Beginning with a backstitch, stitch about 4 in. from a top or bottom edge—one without the scallops. Continue around until you turn the fourth corner. Stitch about 4 in. from that corner, leaving a 4-in. to 6-in. opening. Backstitch.

Trim the seam allowances close to the seam at the corners of the quilt to reduce the bulk.

Turn the quilt right side out. Use a pointed tool to push the corners out neatly. Hand-stitch the opening closed.

QUILT

13. Using a 3.5 to 4.0 machine stitch, stitch the red strips in vertical rows ½ in. apart.

Trace the scallops onto the pink fabric below them. Stitch ½ in. away from the marking to outline the scallops.

10

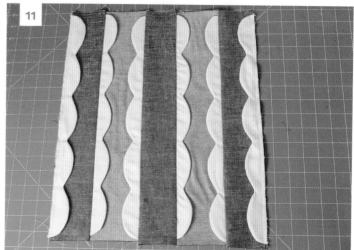

11

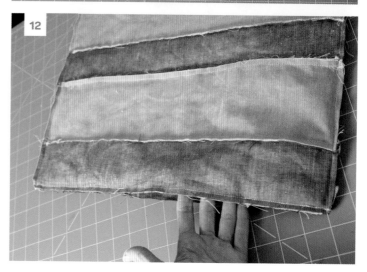

12

Mini
QUILT PILLOW

DESIGNER:
Jayne Davis

The size alone dictates that these mini quilts are perfect candidates for pillows. For my own home, I made pillows using the All Tied Up in Wool pattern (p. 18). For her home, Jodie made pillows using the Hawaiian Gone Modern Stenciled Quilt (p. 14) and the Decorative Stitched Circles pattern (p. 6). Use the pattern that works best for your design needs.

What You'll Need

- **All Tied Up in Wool (p. 18) pattern** or mini quilt pattern of your choice
- 18-in.-square muslin for the quilt backing
- 16½-in.-square fabric for the pillow backing
- 16-in.-square pillow form
- Handful of polyester stuffing
- Seam roll or tightly rolled up towel

MAKE THE QUILT PILLOW

1. Follow the mini quilt directions on p. 19 through tying the quilt together in step 5. Use the muslin square as the backing for the quilt sandwich and do not apply the binding.

   Trim the quilt sandwich to 16½ in. square after tying.

2. Layer the quilt top and pillow backing, right sides together. Match the raw edges.

   Pin together, leaving a wide opening at the bottom to insert the pillow form. Machine-stitch, rounding the corners. The rounded corners will make the pillow look better when finished.

   Turn the pillow cover right side out and carefully press it using a seam roll or a tightly rolled up towel.

3. Fill the four corners tightly with polyester stuffing. Insert the pillow form. Pin the opening at the bottom edge and slipstitch closed.

TEMPLATES

DECORATIVE STITCHED CIRCLES

Enlarge the template by 400 percent, one-quarter of the pattern at a time. Tape the pattern together.

SCALLOPED!

Enlarge the template by 200 percent and make three copies. Cut along the dashed lines. Overlap and tape them together to make a pattern with five scallops.

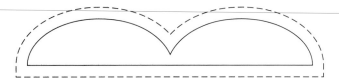

ALL TIED UP IN WOOL

Use at 100 percent.

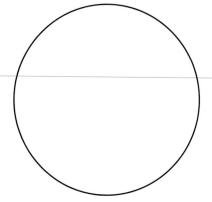

HAWAIIAN GONE MODERN STENCILED QUILT

Enlarge the red flower template by 400 percent and the yellow flower template by 200 percent.

Yellow Flower

Red Flower

Cut a separate stencil for each color.

Place along pressed foldline

Place along pressed foldline

Center of block

METRIC EQUIVALENTS

One inch equals approximately 2.54 centimeters. To convert inches to centimeters, multiply the figure in inches by 2.54 and round off to the nearest half centimeter, or use the chart below, in which figures are rounded off (1 centimeter equals 10 millimeters).

⅛ in. = 3 mm	4 in. = 10 cm	16 in. = 40.5 cm
¼ in. = 6 mm	5 in. = 12.5 cm	18 in. = 45.5 cm
⅜ in. = 1 cm	6 in. = 15 cm	20 in. = 51 cm
½ in. = 1.3 cm	7 in. = 18 cm	21 in. = 53.5 cm
⅝ in. = 1.5 cm	8 in. = 20.5 cm	22 in. = 56 cm
¾ in. = 2 cm	9 in. = 23 cm	24 in. = 61 cm
⅞ in. = 2.2 cm	10 in. = 25.5 cm	25 in. = 63.5 cm
1 in. = 2.5 cm	12 in. = 30.5 cm	36 in. = 92 cm
2 in. = 5 cm	14 in. = 35.5 cm	45 in. = 114.5 cm
3 in. = 7.5 cm	15 in. = 38 cm	60 in. = 152 cm

Look for these other *Threads* Selects booklets at www.tauntonstore.com and wherever crafts are sold.

Small Projects to Quilt
Joan Ford
EAN: 9781627100977
8½ x 10⅞, 32 pages
Product# 078032
$9.95 U.S., $9.95 Can.

Prairie Girl Sewing
Jennifer Worick
EAN: 9781621139508
8½ x 10⅞, 32 pages
Product# 078029
$9.95 U.S., $9.95 Can.

Prairie Girl Gifts
Jennifer Worick
EAN: 9781621139492
8½ x 10⅞, 32 pages
Product # 078030
$9.95 U.S., $9.95 Can.

Easy-to-Sew Pillows
EAN: 9781621138266
8½ x 10⅞, 32 pages
Product# 078019
$9.95 U.S., $9.95 Can.

Easy-to-Sew Tote Bags
EAN: 9781621138297
8½ x 10⅞, 32 pages
Product# 078021
$9.95 U.S., $9.95 Can.

Easy-to-Sew Flowers
EAN: 9781621138259
8½ x 10⅞, 32 pages
Product# 078017
$9.95 U.S., $9.95 Can.

Easy-to-Sew Gifts
EAN: 9781621138310
8½ x 10⅞, 32 pages
Product # 078023
$9.95 U.S., $9.95 Can.

Easy-to-Sew Pet Projects
EAN: 9781621138273
8½ x 10⅞, 32 pages
Product# 078018
$9.95 U.S., $9.95 Can.

Easy-to-Sew Windows
EAN: 9781621138303
8½ x 10⅞, 32 pages
Product# 078022
$9.95 U.S., $9.95 Can.

Easy-to-Sew Handbags
EAN: 9781621138242
8½ x 10⅞, 32 pages
Product# 078016
$9.95 U.S., $9.95 Can.

Easy-to-Sew Kitchen
EAN: 9781621138327
8½ x 10⅞, 32 pages
Product# 078024
$9.95 U.S., $9.95 Can.

Easy-to-Sew Lace
EAN: 9781621138228
8½ x 10⅞, 32 pages
Product# 078014
$9.95 U.S., $9.95 Can.